30 Vegan Recipes for Kids Gluten Free

Vegan Cookbook - Vegan recipes, Volume 2

BDM

Published by BDM, 2023.

30 VEGAN RECIPES FOR KIDS GLUTEN FREE

First edition. October 27, 2023.

ISBN: 979-8227209801

Written by BDM.

30 VEGAN
RECIPES
FOR KIDS
GLUTEN FREE

Welcome to a world of flavor, fun, and nutrition designed especially for the little gourmets at home. This book, "Vegan Gluten-Free Recipes for Kids," is a gateway to a kitchen that combines the goodness of vegan foods with the friendliness of gluten-free recipes, all crafted with love to satisfy the most discerning palates: those of our children.

In an ever-evolving world, many parents are seeking healthier and more ethical food options for their children. The vegan diet, which excludes all animal products, has become an increasingly popular choice. At the same time, gluten sensitivity or intolerance is a common concern, making the need for gluten-free recipes essential.

In this book, we've merged these two needs into a compilation of 30 recipes that blend the wonder of flavors with the promise of healthy and balanced eating. Our goal is to show that vegan gluten-free cooking can be exciting, delicious, and nutritious.

Each recipe has been carefully selected to captivate the imagination of the little ones and to ensure that their taste buds are delighted with every bite. From mini chickpea burgers to gluten-free oatmeal cookies and baked french fries, these dishes are designed with children in mind but are delicious enough to please the entire family.

In addition to the recipes, you'll find useful tips on introducing vegan and gluten-free eating into your children's lives, as well as nutritional information to ensure they're getting all the nutrients they need to grow strong and healthy.

So, parents and caregivers, join us on this culinary journey. Together, we'll explore a world of flavors, textures, and colors that will awaken the imagination and palate of the little gourmets. It's time to cook, learn, and, above all, enjoy!

Get ready to discover the magic of vegan gluten-free cooking for kids. Let's embark on this journey together!

*Introducing Vegan Cuisine into a Child's Life

1. Education and Communication:
- Start by talking to your child about choosing a vegan diet. Explain why you've made this decision and emphasize the positive aspects, such as animal welfare and health.
- Use age-appropriate language to explain concepts like "vegan" and "animal-derived foods."

2. Involve the Child:
- Invite your child to participate in recipe selection and meal preparation. This can be a fun and educational activity that fosters their interest in vegan cooking.
- Visit local farmers' markets and health food stores together to explore vegan ingredients and learn about their origins.

3. Food Diversity:
- Ensure your child's diet is balanced and varied. Include a wide range of fruits, vegetables, legumes, whole grains, nuts, and seeds.
- Gradually introduce new foods and recipes to maintain their interest and avoid dietary monotony.

4. Convert Favorite Dishes:
- Adapt your child's favorite dishes to be vegan. For example, prepare vegan mac 'n' cheese, chickpea burgers, or cheeseless pizza.
- Make the transition gradual by replacing animal-derived ingredients with plant-based alternatives.

5. Maintain a Vegan Environment:
- Create a vegan-friendly home environment by gradually phasing out animal-derived products and replacing them with vegan options.
- Ensure non-vegan foods are out of your child's reach to prevent temptation.

6. Be an Example:

- Model healthy vegan eating habits by setting an example for your child. Enjoy nutritious vegan foods and show enthusiasm for vegan cuisine.

7. Teach Empathy:

- Talk to your child about the importance of treating animals with kindness and respect, which can help foster empathy toward living beings.

- Explain how a vegan diet contributes to animal protection and environmental conservation.

8. Seek Social Support:

- Look for local or online vegan groups or communities where your child can connect with other kids following a similar diet. This can help reduce any feelings of isolation.

9. Consult a Healthcare Professional:

- Before making significant changes to your child's diet, consult with a pediatrician or registered dietitian to ensure they're receiving all the necessary nutrients for healthy growth.

Remember that introducing a vegan diet into a child's life should be a gradual and positive process. Open communication, education, and support are key to helping your child adjust to and enjoy a healthy vegan diet.

Vegan Mini Chickpea Burgers

Ingredients:
- 1 can (400g) of cooked chickpeas, drained and rinsed
- 1/2 red onion, finely chopped
- 2 garlic cloves, minced
- 1 carrot, grated
- 1/2 cup gluten-free rolled oats
- 1 teaspoon ground cumin
- 1 teaspoon smoked paprika
- 1/2 teaspoon ground coriander
- Salt and pepper to taste
- Olive oil for cooking
- Gluten-free burger buns
- Lettuce leaves, tomato slices, and avocado for topping

Instructions:

1. Rinse and drain the chickpeas, and place them in a food processor along with the chopped onion, minced garlic, grated carrot, rolled oats, ground cumin, smoked paprika, ground coriander, salt, and pepper.

2. Process the mixture until it forms a smooth, homogeneous dough. If necessary, you can add a little water to aid in the processing.

3. Divide the dough into portions and shape them into small burger patties, about the size of mini burgers.

4. Heat a non-stick skillet with a little olive oil over medium-high heat.

5. Cook the mini vegan chickpea burgers for approximately 4-5 minutes on each side, or until they are golden brown and crispy.

6. Serve the burgers in gluten-free burger buns, topped with lettuce leaves, tomato slices, avocado, and any other condiments you like.

Cooking Tips:

- Ensure that the dough is compact enough to allow the burgers to maintain their shape while cooking.

- You can refrigerate the dough for about 30 minutes before forming the burgers to make it easier to handle.

- If you prefer, you can also bake the burgers at 180°C (350°F) for 20-25 minutes instead of cooking them in the skillet.

Tips for Kids:

- Let the kids help you shape the burgers! They'll enjoy participating in the kitchen.

- Encourage them to personalize their burgers with their favorite toppings, such as avocado, ketchup, mustard, or pickles.

Nutritional Information (per burger, excluding buns and condiments):

- Calories: Approximately 100-120 kcal
- Protein: Approximately 4-5 g
- Fiber: Approximately 4-5 g
- Fat: Approximately 2-3 g
- Carbohydrates: Approximately 16-18 g

These vegan mini chickpea burgers are a delicious and nutritious option for both kids and adults. They are rich in protein and fiber, making them an excellent alternative to traditional burgers. Enjoy this tasty and healthy meal!

Vegan Macaroni and Cheese (Dairy-Free)

Ingredients:

- 2 cups gluten-free macaroni (you can use another gluten-free pasta if preferred)
- 2 medium carrots, peeled and chopped into pieces
- 1 medium potato, peeled and chopped into pieces
- 1/2 cup raw cashews
- 1/4 cup nutritional yeast
- 2 tablespoons olive oil
- 2 cloves garlic, minced
- 1 teaspoon Dijon mustard
- 1 teaspoon apple cider vinegar
- Salt and pepper to taste

Instructions:

1. Cook the macaroni according to the package instructions in salted water until al dente. Then, drain and set aside.

2. In a large saucepan, boil the carrots and potatoes until they are tender. This will take approximately 10-15 minutes.

3. While the carrots and potatoes are cooking, place the cashews in a cup with boiling water for about 10 minutes to soften them.

4. Drain the cashews and place them in a high-powered blender along with the cooked carrots, potatoes, nutritional yeast, olive oil, minced garlic, Dijon mustard, and apple cider vinegar.

5. Process the mixture until it becomes smooth and creamy. If needed, add a bit of water to achieve the desired texture.

6. Pour the vegan cheese sauce over the cooked macaroni and mix well.

7. Heat the pasta over medium heat for a few minutes until the sauce is hot. Season with salt and pepper to taste.

8. Serve the hot vegan macaroni and cheese.

Cooking Tips:

- You can adjust the sauce's consistency by adding more water for a thinner texture or more cashews for a richer flavor.

- For extra flavor, consider adding onion powder, turmeric, or paprika to the vegan cheese sauce.

Tips for Kids:

- Encourage kids to help in the kitchen, especially with mixing the sauce and pasta.

- Decorate the macaroni and cheese with a bit of chopped parsley or cherry tomato slices to make it more appealing to children.

Nutritional Information (per serving):

- Calories: Approximately 350-400 kcal

- Protein: Approximately 10-12 g

- Fiber: Approximately 5-6 g

- Fat: Approximately 15-18 g

- Carbohydrates: Approximately 45-50 g

This vegan macaroni and cheese is a delicious and dairy-free option for both kids and adults. It's rich in protein and fiber, making it a comforting and nutritious dish. Enjoy this vegan and healthy twist on a classic favorite!

Plant-Based Vegan Chicken Nuggets

Ingredients:

- 1 cup textured soy protein (TSP)
- 1 cup hot water
- 1/2 cup breadcrumbs (ensure it's gluten-free if needed)
- 1/4 cup chickpea flour
- 1 teaspoon garlic powder
- 1 teaspoon onion powder
- 1/2 teaspoon paprika
- 1/2 teaspoon dried thyme
- Salt and pepper to taste
- Vegetable oil for frying

Instructions:

1. In a large bowl, place the textured soy protein (TSP) and pour the hot water over it. Cover and let it sit for about 10 minutes or until the TSP is hydrated.

2. Drain any excess water from the hydrated TSP.

3. Add breadcrumbs, chickpea flour, garlic powder, onion powder, paprika, dried thyme, salt, and pepper to the hydrated TSP. Mix well until you have a uniform dough.

4. Form small portions of the dough into nugget shapes.

5. Heat a skillet with vegetable oil over medium-high heat.

6. Fry the plant-based vegan chicken nuggets in the hot oil until they are golden brown and crispy on both sides, approximately 3-4 minutes per side.

7. Drain the nuggets on paper towels to remove excess oil.

Cooking Tips:

- You can adjust the spices and herbs according to your personal preferences. Adding a touch of cayenne or ground black pepper can give them a bit of spiciness if you like.

Tips for Kids:

- Get kids involved in the preparation! Letting them help shape the nuggets can be fun and educational.

- Serve the nuggets with a variety of vegan dipping sauces, such as vegan ketchup, mustard, or coconut yogurt-based sauce.

Nutritional Information (per serving, approximate):

- Calories: Approximately 80-100 kcal per nugget (depending on size)

- Protein: Approximately 7-9 g per nugget

- Fiber: Approximately 2-3 g per nugget

- Fat: Approximately 2-3 g per nugget

- Carbohydrates: Approximately 8-10 g per nugget

These Plant-Based Vegan Chicken Nuggets are a delicious and nutritious alternative to traditional chicken nuggets. They are rich in protein and low in saturated fats, making them a healthier choice. Enjoy this vegan recipe!

Gluten-Free Vegan Mini Pizzas

Ingredients for the Crust:
- 1 cup almond flour
- 1/4 cup coconut flour
- 2 tablespoons flaxseed meal
- 1 teaspoon gluten-free baking powder
- 1/2 teaspoon salt
- 1/2 cup water
- 2 tablespoons olive oil

Topping Ingredients:
- Gluten-free tomato sauce
- Chopped vegetables (such as tomatoes, mushrooms, bell peppers, spinach, etc.)
- Gluten-free vegan cheese (optional)
- Oregano and other dried herbs for seasoning

Instructions:

1. Preheat the oven to 180°C (350°F) and line a baking tray with parchment paper.

2. In a large bowl, mix the almond flour, coconut flour, flaxseed meal, gluten-free baking powder, and salt.

3. Add water and olive oil to the flour mixture and stir well to form a homogeneous dough.

4. Divide the dough into small portions and shape thin disks on the prepared baking tray. These will be the pizza crusts.

5. Bake the pizza crusts for about 10-12 minutes, or until they are lightly golden.

6. Remove the pizza crusts from the oven and let them cool for a few minutes.

7. Once the crusts are ready, spread a layer of gluten-free tomato sauce on each one.

8. Add the chopped vegetables and, if desired, gluten-free vegan cheese.

9. Sprinkle with oregano and other dried herbs to your taste.

10. Bake the mini pizzas in the oven for another 10-12 minutes, or until the ingredients are well-cooked and the vegan cheese melts (if using).

Cooking Tips:

- Make sure to use gluten-free almond flour, coconut flour, and baking powder if you want the recipe to be entirely gluten-free.

- You can customize the mini pizzas with your favorite toppings, such as olives, red onion, jalapeños, etc.

Tips for Kids:

- Let kids help prepare their own mini pizzas. It can be fun and allows them to choose their favorite toppings.

- Mini pizzas are perfect for kids' parties or as an after-school snack.

Nutritional Information (per mini pizza, approximate):

- Calories: Approximately 100-120 kcal

- Protein: Approximately 3-4 g

- Fiber: Approximately 2-3 g
- Fat: Approximately 7-8 g
- Carbohydrates: Approximately 7-8 g

These Gluten-Free Vegan Mini Pizzas are a delicious and healthy option for both kids and adults. They are rich in protein and fiber, and the crust is made from almond and coconut flour, making them suitable for those following a gluten-free diet. Enjoy these mini pizzas as a tasty and worry-free snack!

Vegan Lentil "Meat" Tacos

Ingredients for Lentil "Meat":
    - 1 cup dry lentils (green or brown), rinsed and drained
    - 3 cups water
    - 1 tablespoon olive oil
    - 1 onion, chopped
    - 2 cloves garlic, minced
    - 1 large carrot, peeled and diced
    - 1 teaspoon ground cumin
    - 1 teaspoon smoked paprika
    - 1/2 teaspoon chili powder (adjust to desired spiciness)
    - Salt and pepper to taste
    - 1 can (400 g) crushed tomatoes (no salt added)
    - 1/2 cup vegetable broth
    - Juice of 1 lemon
    Ingredients for Tacos:
    - Corn or wheat tortillas (make sure they are vegan and gluten-free if necessary)
    - Chopped lettuce
    - Diced tomatoes
    - Thinly sliced red onion
    - Avocado slices
    - Hot sauce (optional)
    - Fresh cilantro (optional)

Instructions:

1. Rinse the lentils and cook them in 3 cups of boiling water for about 20-25 minutes, or until they are tender but not mushy. Then, drain them and set aside.

2. In a large skillet, heat the olive oil over medium heat. Add the chopped onion and minced garlic, and sauté until they are golden brown.

3. Add the diced carrot to the skillet and cook for a few minutes until it softens.

4. Add the cooked lentils, ground cumin, smoked paprika, chili powder, salt, and pepper to the skillet. Cook for a few minutes to blend the flavors.

5. Pour the crushed tomatoes and vegetable broth into the skillet and mix well. Cook over medium heat for about 10-15 minutes, or until the mixture thickens and is properly cooked.

6. Add the lemon juice and stir. Adjust the seasoning if necessary.

7. Heat the tortillas according to the package instructions.

8. Fill the tortillas with the lentil "meat" and add lettuce, tomatoes, red onion, avocado, hot sauce (if using), and fresh cilantro according to your preferences.

9. Serve the Vegan Lentil "Meat" Tacos and enjoy!

Cooking Tips:

- If you prefer a smoother consistency for the lentil "meat," you can use an immersion blender to partially blend the mixture.

Tips for Kids:

- Let kids help assemble their own tacos. They'll love choosing their favorite ingredients and customizing their tacos.

Nutritional Information (per serving, approximate):

- Calories: Approximately 250-300 kcal (excluding tortillas)

- Protein: Approximately 12-15 g

- Fiber: Approximately 8-10 g

- Fat: Approximately 5-7 g

- Carbohydrates: Approximately 40-45 g

These Vegan Lentil "Meat" Tacos are a delicious and healthy option. They are rich in protein and fiber, and lentils provide a good amount of iron and other essential nutrients. We hope you enjoy this vegan recipe for your meals!

Vegan Tomato Soup with Grilled Cheese

Ingredients for Tomato Soup:
- 1 tablespoon olive oil
- 1 onion, chopped
- 2 cloves garlic, minced
- 1 can (14 oz) crushed tomatoes (no salt added)
- 2 cups vegetable broth
- 1 teaspoon sugar
- 1 teaspoon dried basil
- Salt and pepper to taste
- 1/2 cup almond milk (or any plant-based milk of your choice)
- 2 tablespoons nutritional yeast (optional, for a cheesy flavor)
- 2 tablespoons cornstarch dissolved in 2 tablespoons water (to thicken the soup)

Ingredients for Grilled Cheese:
- Gluten-free bread (make sure it's vegan and gluten-free if necessary)
- Vegan cheese slices (make sure it's vegan and gluten-free if necessary)
- Coconut oil or vegan margarine (for grilling)

Instructions:

For the Tomato Soup:

1. In a large pot, heat the olive oil over medium heat. Add the chopped onion and minced garlic, and sauté until they become golden brown.

2. Add the crushed tomatoes, vegetable broth, sugar, and dried basil to the pot. Bring the mixture to a boil, then reduce the heat and simmer for about 15-20 minutes.

3. Use an immersion blender or a high-powered blender to blend the soup until it's smooth and creamy.

4. Return the soup to the pot and heat it over medium heat. Add the almond milk and nutritional yeast (if using). Mix well.

5. Add the cornstarch-water mixture to thicken the soup. Cook for a few minutes until the soup becomes thicker. Season with salt and pepper to taste.

For Grilled Cheese:

1. Place the vegan cheese slices between two slices of bread.

2. Heat a large skillet over medium heat and melt a little coconut oil or vegan margarine in it.

3. Place the Grilled Cheese sandwich in the hot skillet and cook until the bread is golden brown and the cheese is melted.

4. Flip the sandwich and cook the other side until it's golden brown and the cheese is completely melted.

Cooking Tips:

- You can customize the soup by adding fresh herbs like basil or chopped parsley before serving.

Kids' Tips:

- Kids can help assemble the Grilled Cheese sandwich, but make sure to supervise them when using the hot skillet.

Nutritional Information (per serving of soup, approximate):

- Calories: Approximately 150-200 kcal

- Protein: Approximately 2-3 g

- Fiber: Approximately 3-4 g

- Fat: Approximately 7-8 g

- Carbohydrates: Approximately 20-25 g

This Vegan Tomato Soup with Grilled Cheese is a delicious and comforting meal. The soup is packed with tomato flavors, and the vegan Grilled Cheese version adds a special touch. Plus, it's a gluten-free option for those with dietary restrictions. We hope you enjoy this recipe!

Baked Potato Fries with Pea Dip

Ingredients for Potato Fries:
- 4 medium potatoes, peeled and cut into thin strips
- 2 tablespoons olive oil
- Salt and pepper to taste
- 1/2 teaspoon paprika (optional, for flavor)

Ingredients for Pea Dip:
- 1 cup peas (fresh or frozen, cooked and drained)
- 1 garlic clove, minced
- 2 tablespoons lemon juice
- 2 tablespoons tahini (sesame paste)
- 2 tablespoons olive oil
- Salt and pepper to taste
- Water (to adjust consistency)

Instructions:
For the Potato Fries:
1. Preheat the oven to 220°C (425°F) and line a baking sheet with parchment paper.

2. In a large bowl, toss the potato strips with olive oil, salt, pepper, and paprika (if using). Ensure the potatoes are well coated.

3. Place the potato strips on the prepared baking sheet in a single layer, making sure they are not overcrowded.

4. Bake the potatoes in the preheated oven for approximately 25-30 minutes or until they are golden and crispy. You can flip them halfway through the cooking time for even cooking.

5. Remove the fries from the oven and allow them to cool slightly before serving.

For the Pea Dip:

1. In a blender or food processor, combine the cooked peas, minced garlic, lemon juice, tahini, olive oil, salt, and pepper.

2. Blend everything at high speed until you achieve a smooth mixture. If needed, add a little water to adjust the dip's consistency until it's creamy and easy to dip into.

3. Taste and adjust the seasoning according to your preference.

Cooking Tips:

- You can customize the potato fries by adding your favorite seasonings, such as garlic powder, paprika, or even vegan grated cheese after baking.

Nutritional Information (per serving, approximate):

- Calories: Approximately 150-200 kcal (excluding the dip)
- Protein: Approximately 3-4 g
- Fiber: Approximately 4-5 g
- Fat: Approximately 6-7 g
- Carbohydrates: Approximately 20-25 g

These Baked Potato Fries with Pea Dip are a healthier alternative to traditional fried potato fries, as they are baked instead of fried. The pea dip adds a refreshing and flavorful touch to this snack. We hope you enjoy this delicious recipe!

Vegan French Toast (Egg and Dairy-Free)

Ingredients:
- 4 slices of bread (make sure it's vegan and dairy-free)
- 1 cup almond milk (or any plant-based milk of your choice)
- 2 tablespoons chickpea flour
- 1 tablespoon sugar
- 1 teaspoon vanilla extract
- 1/2 teaspoon ground cinnamon
- Pinch of salt
- Coconut oil or vegan margarine (for greasing the pan)

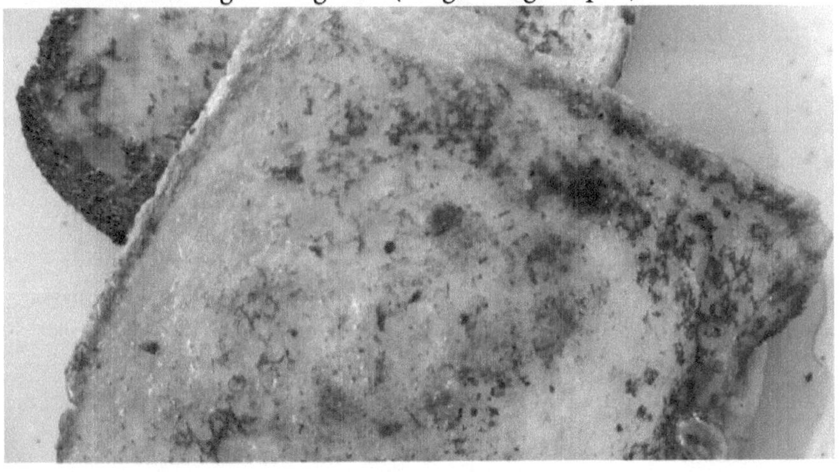

Instructions:

1. In a bowl, mix almond milk, chickpea flour, sugar, vanilla extract, ground cinnamon, and a pinch of salt. Whisk well until all ingredients are fully combined.

2. Heat a large skillet over medium heat and add a little coconut oil or vegan margarine to grease it.

3. Dip each slice of bread into the liquid mixture you prepared, ensuring they are well coated but not soaked.

4. Cook the bread slices in the hot skillet for about 2-3 minutes on each side, or until they are golden and crispy.

5. Remove the French toasts from the pan and place them on a plate. You can sprinkle a bit more sugar and cinnamon on top if desired.

Cooking Tips:

- Add your favorite toppings like fresh fruit, maple syrup, or powdered sugar for an extra flavor boost.

Nutritional Information (per serving, approximate):

- Calories: Approximately 150-200 kcal (excluding toppings)

- Protein: Approximately 4-5 g

- Fiber: Approximately 2-3 g

- Fat: Approximately 5-6 g

- Carbohydrates: Approximately 25-30 g

These Vegan French Toasts are a delicious option for a vegan and dairy-free breakfast or brunch. They contain no eggs or dairy and are perfect for those following a vegan lifestyle. We hope you enjoy this healthy and tasty recipe!

Vegan Hot Dogs with Mustard and Ketchup Sauce

Ingredients:
- 4 vegan sausages (ensure they are vegan and contain no animal ingredients)
- 4 vegan hot dog buns (verify they are vegan)
- 2 tablespoons vegan mustard
- 2 tablespoons vegan ketchup
- 1 red onion, thinly sliced into rings
- 1/4 cup sliced pickles
- 1/4 cup shredded cabbage
- 1/4 cup chopped green onions (optional)
- Vegetable oil (for grilling the sausages)
- Salt and pepper to taste

Instructions:
1. Preheat a grill or non-stick skillet over medium-high heat.

2. While the grill is heating, you can warm the hot dog buns in the oven or toaster until they're golden.

3. Grill the vegan sausages for about 5-7 minutes, turning them occasionally until they are heated through and have grill marks.

4. While the sausages are cooking, prepare your hot dog toppings. You can chop the onions, pickles, cabbage, and green onions if you haven't done so already.

5. Once the sausages are ready, place them inside the hot dog buns.

6. Add mustard, ketchup, and your favorite toppings on top of the sausages.

7. Season with salt and pepper to taste.

8. Serve your Vegan Hot Dogs with Mustard and Ketchup Sauce alongside fries, a salad, or any side you prefer.

Cooking Tips:

- You can customize your vegan hot dogs with other condiments and ingredients like avocado, jalapeños, or vegan cheese.

Nutritional Information (per hot dog, approximate):

- Calories: Approximately 250-300 kcal (excluding sides)

- Protein: Approximately 10-12 g

- Fiber: Approximately 3-4 g

- Fat: Approximately 10-12 g

- Carbohydrates: Approximately 25-30 g

These Vegan Hot Dogs with Mustard and Ketchup Sauce are a delicious and animal-free alternative to traditional hot dogs. They're easy to prepare and perfect for a quick and tasty meal. We hope you enjoy this recipe!

Carrot Sticks with Hummus

Ingredients:
- 4-5 large carrots, peeled and cut into long strips (approximately 4-5 inches in length)
    - 1 cup cooked chickpeas (canned or homemade)
    - 2 tablespoons tahini (sesame paste)
    - 2 tablespoons lemon juice
    - 2 cloves of garlic, chopped
    - 2 tablespoons olive oil
    - 1/2 teaspoon ground cumin
    - Salt and pepper to taste
    - Water (to adjust consistency)
    - Pinch of smoked paprika (optional, for garnish)

Instructions:
For the Carrot Sticks:
1. Wash, peel, and cut the carrots into long strips, resembling sticks.
2. You can either boil the carrot strips in water for a few minutes until they are tender but still crisp, or serve them raw, depending on your preference.
For the Hummus:

1. In a blender or food processor, combine the cooked chickpeas, tahini, lemon juice, chopped garlic, olive oil, ground cumin, salt, and pepper.

2. Blend all the ingredients at high speed until you achieve a smooth mixture. If needed, add a little water to adjust the hummus's consistency until it's creamy and easy to dip into.

3. Taste and adjust the seasoning according to your preference.

To Serve:

1. Place the hummus in a bowl and sprinkle a pinch of smoked paprika on top, if desired.

2. Serve the carrot sticks with hummus on a plate or platter.

Cooking Tips:

- You can customize the hummus by adding ingredients like black olives, roasted red peppers, or cilantro for different flavors.

Nutritional Information (per serving, approximate):

- Calories: Approximately 150-200 kcal (excluding smoked paprika)

- Protein: Approximately 4-5 g

- Fiber: Approximately 5-6 g

- Fat: Approximately 7-8 g

- Carbohydrates: Approximately 15-20 g

These Carrot Sticks with Hummus are a healthy and delicious snack. The carrots provide a fresh and crunchy element, while the hummus is a smooth and flavorful dip. We hope you enjoy this recipe as a snack or appetizer!

Vegan Mini Potato Pancakes

Ingredients:
- 2 medium potatoes, peeled and grated
- 1 small onion, finely chopped
- 1/4 cup chickpea flour
- 1/4 cup whole wheat flour (make sure it's vegan)
- 1 teaspoon baking powder
- 1/2 teaspoon ground cumin
- 1/2 teaspoon ground turmeric
- Salt and pepper to taste
- Vegetable oil for frying

Instructions:

1. In a large bowl, combine the grated potatoes and finely chopped onion.

2. In another bowl, mix the chickpea flour, whole wheat flour, baking powder, ground cumin, ground turmeric, salt, and pepper.

3. Add the flour mixture to the potatoes and onions and stir well until all the ingredients are thoroughly combined. You should have a thick batter.

4. Heat a large skillet with vegetable oil over medium-high heat.

5. Using a spoon, place small portions of the batter in the hot skillet and press them lightly to form the mini pancakes. Cook until they are golden and crispy on both sides, which should take about 3-4 minutes per side.

6. Remove the mini pancakes from the skillet and place them on a plate lined with paper towels to absorb any excess oil.

7. Serve hot, accompanied by your favorite vegan sauce or dressing.

Cooking Tips:

- You can add additional ingredients to the mixture, such as chopped spinach, bell peppers, or corn, to vary the flavor and texture.

Nutritional Information (per serving, approximate):

- Calories: Approximately 80-100 kcal for every 3-4 mini pancakes

- Protein: Approximately 2-3 g

- Fiber: Approximately 2-3 g

- Fat: Approximately 1-2 g

- Carbohydrates: Approximately 15-20 g

These Vegan Mini Potato Pancakes are a delicious appetizer or side dish that you can enjoy anytime. They are crispy on the outside and soft on the inside, and their flavor is delightful. We hope you enjoy this recipe!

Peanut Butter and Banana Sandwiches

Ingredients:
- 4 slices of whole wheat bread (make sure it's vegan)
- 2 ripe bananas, sliced
- 4 tablespoons of peanut butter (make sure it's vegan)
- 1 teaspoon of vegan honey (optional)
- 1 tablespoon of chia seeds (optional)
- 1 tablespoon of chopped almonds or walnuts (optional)
- A pinch of cinnamon (optional)

Instructions:

1. Spread one tablespoon of peanut butter on each of the four slices of bread.

2. Place the banana slices onto two of the bread slices, making sure to distribute them evenly.

3. If desired, you can drizzle a small amount of vegan honey over the bananas for a touch of sweetness.

4. Sprinkle chia seeds and chopped almonds or walnuts over the bananas to add texture and nutrition.

5. If you like, add a pinch of cinnamon for flavor.

6. Cover the peanut butter-covered bread slices with the banana-covered bread slices to form two sandwiches.

7. Gently press the sandwiches and cut them into your preferred shape, whether it's triangles, quarters, or simply halves.

Cooking Tips:

- You can customize these sandwiches by adding ingredients like berries, raisins, vegan chocolate chips, or shredded coconut.

Nutritional Information (per sandwich, approximate):

- Calories: Approximately 300-350 kcal (depending on optional ingredients)

- Protein: Approximately 7-8 g

- Fiber: Approximately 7-8 g

- Fat: Approximately 12-15 g

- Carbohydrates: Approximately 40-45 g

These Peanut Butter and Banana Sandwiches are a delicious snack that combines the creaminess of peanut butter with the sweetness of bananas. They are a nutritious and flavorful option for a quick breakfast or snack. We hope you enjoy this recipe!

Vegan Mini Bean and Rice Burritos

Ingredients:
- 4 whole wheat tortillas (ensure they are vegan)
- 1 cup cooked brown rice
- 1 cup cooked black beans
- 1 cup sweet corn (canned or frozen)
- 1 cup fresh tomato, chopped
- 1/2 cup red onion, chopped
- 1/2 cup avocado, cubed
- 1 teaspoon ground cumin
- 1 teaspoon smoked paprika
- 1/2 teaspoon garlic powder
- Salt and pepper to taste
- Hot sauce (optional, to taste)
- Lettuce leaves (for serving, optional)

Instructions:

1. In a large bowl, mix the cooked brown rice, cooked black beans, sweet corn, chopped tomato, chopped red onion, cubed avocado, ground cumin, smoked paprika, garlic powder, salt, and pepper. You can add hot sauce if you prefer a little spice.

2. Heat the whole wheat tortillas in a hot skillet or in the microwave for a few seconds to make them more pliable.

3. Place a portion of the rice and bean mixture in the center of each tortilla.

4. Fold the ends of the tortilla inwards, and then roll it up from the bottom, ensuring that the ingredients are well wrapped.

5. You can serve the mini burritos as they are or heat them in a skillet for a few minutes to lightly brown the exterior.

6. Optionally, serve with lettuce leaves as a side.

Cooking Tips:

- You can customize your mini burritos by adding ingredients like avocado, bell peppers, cilantro, or jalapeños to give them different flavors and textures.

Nutritional Information (per mini burrito, approximate):

- Calories: Approximately 200-250 kcal (depending on ingredients and size)

- Protein: Approximately 6-8 g

- Fiber: Approximately 5-7 g

- Fat: Approximately 5-7 g

- Carbohydrates: Approximately 30-35 g

These Vegan Mini Bean and Rice Burritos are a delicious and versatile option for lunch, dinner, or a snack. They are easy to prepare and can be customized according to your preferences. We hope you enjoy this recipe!

Crispy Tofu Nuggets

Ingredients:

- 1 block of firm tofu (14 oz or 400 g), well-drained and cut into small pieces
    - 1 cup of breadcrumbs (make sure they're vegan)
    - 1/2 cup of all-purpose flour (or gluten-free flour if preferred)
    - 1 teaspoon of garlic powder
    - 1 teaspoon of onion powder
    - 1 teaspoon of smoked paprika
    - Salt and pepper to taste
    - 1 cup of plant-based milk (such as almond or soy milk)
    - Vegetable oil for frying

Instructions:

1. Prepare a plate with the all-purpose flour and another with the plant-based milk.

2. In a third plate, mix the breadcrumbs with garlic powder, onion powder, smoked paprika, salt, and pepper.

3. Dip each piece of tofu into the all-purpose flour to coat it, then dip it into the plant-based milk, and finally, coat it with the breadcrumb mixture.

4. Heat enough vegetable oil in a large skillet over medium-high heat.

5. Once the oil is hot, place the tofu nuggets in the skillet and fry them until they are golden and crispy on all sides, which should take about 3-4 minutes per side.

6. Remove the tofu nuggets and place them on a plate lined with paper towels to remove excess oil.

7. Serve hot, accompanied by your favorite vegan dipping sauces.

Cooking Tips:

- You can customize the tofu nuggets by adding additional spices or herbs to the breadcrumb mixture, such as oregano, thyme, or cayenne pepper.

Nutritional Information (per serving, approximate):

- Calories: Approximately 150-200 kcal for 3-4 nuggets
- Protein: Approximately 10-12 g
- Fiber: Approximately 2-3 g
- Fat: Approximately 6-8 g
- Carbohydrates: Approximately 15-20 g

These Crispy Tofu Nuggets are a delicious vegan alternative to conventional chicken nuggets. They are crispy on the outside and tender on the inside, and you can enjoy them with your favorite dipping sauces. We hope you enjoy this recipe!

Vegan Fruit Salad with Chocolate Sauce

Ingredients:
   For the fruit salad:
   - 2 cups of strawberries, washed and sliced
   - 2 ripe bananas, sliced
   - 1 cup of seedless grapes, halved
   - 1 orange, peeled and segmented
   - 1 apple, diced
   - 1 cup of kiwis, peeled and sliced
   - 1 cup of melon, balled or diced
   - 1 cup of pineapple, cubed
   - 1/2 cup of blueberries (optional)
   For the vegan chocolate sauce:
   - 1/4 cup unsweetened cocoa powder
   - 1/4 cup maple syrup or agave syrup
   - 2 tablespoons almond milk (or other plant-based milk)
   - 1/2 teaspoon vanilla extract

Instructions:

1. In a large bowl, combine all the sliced fruits to make the fruit salad. If desired, add the blueberries.

2. In a separate bowl, mix the cocoa powder, maple syrup, almond milk, and vanilla extract to create the vegan chocolate sauce. Adjust the consistency by adding more milk if needed.

3. Drizzle the chocolate sauce over the fruit salad and gently toss to coat all the fruits with the sauce.

4. Serve the vegan fruit salad with chocolate sauce immediately. You can refrigerate any leftovers, but keep in mind that fresh fruits tend to soften over time.

Cooking Tips:

- You can customize your fruit salad by using your favorite fruits or seasonal choices.

Nutritional Information (per serving, approximate):

- Calories: Approximately 150-200 kcal

- Protein: Approximately 2-3 g

- Fiber: Approximately 5-6 g

- Fat: Approximately 1-2 g

- Carbohydrates: Approximately 35-45 g

This Vegan Fruit Salad with Chocolate Sauce is a refreshing and delightful option for dessert or a snack. The vegan chocolate sauce adds a special touch and will satisfy your sweet cravings in a healthy way. We hope you enjoy this recipe!

Zucchini Noodles with Vegan Meatballs

Ingredients:
    For the zucchini noodles:
    - 3-4 medium zucchinis
    - 1 tablespoon of olive oil
    - Salt and pepper to taste
    For the vegan meatballs:
    - 1 can (15 oz or 425 g) of cooked chickpeas, drained and rinsed
    - 1/2 cup of oats (ensure it's gluten-free if necessary)
    - 1/4 cup of chopped onion
    - 2 cloves of garlic, minced
    - 1 teaspoon of ground cumin
    - 1 teaspoon of smoked paprika
    - 1/2 teaspoon of dried oregano
    - Salt and pepper to taste
    - 1 tablespoon of soy sauce (ensure it's gluten-free if necessary)
    - Cooking oil for frying
    For the tomato sauce:
    - 1 can (14 oz or 400 g) of crushed tomatoes
    - 2 cloves of garlic, minced
    - 1 teaspoon of dried basil
    - 1 teaspoon of dried oregano
    - Salt and pepper to taste

Instructions:

For the zucchini noodles:

1. Wash the zucchinis and use a spiralizer or a julienne peeler to create zucchini noodles.

2. Heat the olive oil in a large skillet and sauté the zucchini noodles for about 3-4 minutes or until they are tender. Season with salt and pepper to taste.

For the vegan meatballs:

1. Rinse the chickpeas and place them in a food processor along with the oats, chopped onion, minced garlic, ground cumin, smoked paprika, dried oregano, salt, pepper, and soy sauce.

2. Process until you have a uniform mixture. If the mixture is too wet, you can add a bit more oats.

3. Form small meatballs from the mixture and place them on a tray.

4. Heat a bit of oil in a pan and fry the meatballs until they are golden brown on all sides.

For the tomato sauce:

1. In a pan, sauté the minced garlic in a little oil until fragrant.

2. Add the crushed tomatoes, dried basil, dried oregano, salt, and pepper. Simmer for 10-15 minutes to thicken the sauce.

To serve:

1. Place the zucchini noodles on a plate, add the vegan meatballs, and pour the tomato sauce on top.

2. Optionally, sprinkle with a little nutritional yeast or vegan cheese.

Cooking Tips:

- You can add your favorite herbs and spices to the vegan meatballs for extra flavor.

Nutritional Information (per serving, approximate):

- Calories: Approximately 250-300 kcal

- Protein: Approximately 10-12 g

- Fiber: Approximately 6-8 g

- Fat: Approximately 6-8 g

- Carbohydrates: Approximately 40-45 g

This Zucchini Noodles with Vegan Meatballs dish is a healthy and delicious option that allows you to enjoy the flavors of gluten-free pasta and vegan meatballs. We hope you enjoy this recipe!

Vegan Banana Muffins

Ingredients:
- 3 ripe bananas, mashed
- 1/4 cup vegetable oil
- 1/4 cup brown sugar
- 1/4 cup granulated sugar
- 2 cups all-purpose flour (ensure it's gluten-free if necessary)
- 1 teaspoon baking soda
- 1 teaspoon baking powder
- 1/2 teaspoon salt
- 1/2 teaspoon ground cinnamon
- 1/4 teaspoon nutmeg
- 1/4 cup almond milk (or other plant-based milk)
- 1 teaspoon vanilla extract
- 1/2 cup chopped walnuts (optional)

Instructions:

1. Preheat your oven to 350°F (180°C) and line a muffin tin with parchment paper liners.

2. In a large bowl, combine the mashed bananas, vegetable oil, brown sugar, and granulated sugar. Mix well.

3. In another bowl, sift the flour, baking soda, baking powder, salt, cinnamon, and nutmeg.

4. Add the dry ingredients to the wet ingredients and stir until just combined. Do not overmix; just mix enough to incorporate the flour.

5. Add the almond milk and vanilla extract, and mix until you have a smooth batter.

6. If you wish, add the chopped walnuts and stir.

7. Fill each muffin cup with the batter, filling them about 2/3 full.

8. Bake in the preheated oven for 20-25 minutes or until the muffins are golden and a toothpick inserted into the center comes out clean.

9. Let them cool in the muffin tin for a few minutes, then transfer the muffins to a cooling rack to cool completely.

Cooking Tips:

- You can customize the muffins by adding vegan chocolate chips or raisins instead of walnuts if you prefer.

Nutritional Information (per muffin, approximate):

- Calories: Approximately 180-220 kcal

- Protein: Approximately 2-3 g

- Fiber: Approximately 2-3 g

- Fat: Approximately 8-10 g

- Carbohydrates: Approximately 28-32 g

These delicious Vegan Banana Muffins are a perfect way to use up those ripe bananas. They're great for breakfast or a snack. We hope you enjoy this recipe!

Vegan Spinach Mini Empanadas

Ingredients:
  For the dough:
  - 2 cups of all-purpose flour (ensure it's gluten-free if necessary)
  - 1/2 cup of vegetable oil
  - 1/2 cup of cold water
  - 1/2 teaspoon of salt
  For the filling:
  - 2 cups of fresh spinach, chopped
  - 1 small onion, chopped
  - 2 cloves of garlic, chopped
  - 1 tablespoon of olive oil
  - 1/2 cup of firm tofu, crumbled
  - 1/4 cup of almond milk (or other plant-based milk)
  - Salt and pepper to taste
  - 1/4 cup of nutritional yeast (optional)
  - 1 teaspoon of ground cumin
  - 1/2 teaspoon of turmeric powder (optional, for color)

Instructions:
For the dough:
1. In a large bowl, mix the flour and salt. Add the vegetable oil and mix until the mixture has a sandy texture.

2. Add the cold water and mix until the dough forms. You may need a bit more or less water, so add it gradually.

3. Divide the dough into small portions and form walnut-sized balls.

4. Roll out each ball into a thin circle to form the base of the empanadas.

For the filling:

1. In a large skillet, heat the olive oil over medium heat. Add the onion and garlic, and sauté until they're golden.

2. Add the chopped spinach and sauté until wilted.

3. Add the crumbled tofu, almond milk, salt, pepper, nutritional yeast, ground cumin, and turmeric (if using). Cook for a few minutes until everything is well combined and heated.

To assemble the empanadas:

1. Place a spoonful of the filling in the center of each dough circle.

2. Fold the circle in half to cover the filling and form an empanada. Seal the edges by pressing with a fork.

3. Place the empanadas on a baking tray lined with parchment paper.

4. Bake in a preheated oven at 350°F (180°C) for approximately 20-25 minutes or until they are golden brown.

Cooking Tips:

- You can customize the empanada filling with additional ingredients like chopped olives or red bell pepper.

Nutritional Information (per empanada, approximate):

- Calories: Approximately 120-150 kcal

- Protein: Approximately 3-4 g

- Fiber: Approximately 2-3 g

- Fat: Approximately 6-7 g

- Carbohydrates: Approximately 12-15 g

These Vegan Spinach Mini Empanadas are great as an appetizer or snack. They are a delicious and healthy option to satisfy your cravings. We hope you enjoy this recipe!

Vegan Sushi Rolls

Ingredients:

For the sushi rice:

- 1 cup of sushi rice
- 2 cups of water
- 1/4 cup of rice vinegar
- 2 tablespoons of sugar
- 1/2 teaspoon of salt

For the rolls:

- 1 sheet of nori seaweed
- 1/2 avocado, sliced into strips
- 1/2 cucumber, sliced into strips
- 1/2 carrot, thinly sliced
- 1/4 avocado, sliced into strips
- Soy sauce (make sure it's gluten-free if needed)
- Wasabi (optional)
- Pickled ginger (optional)

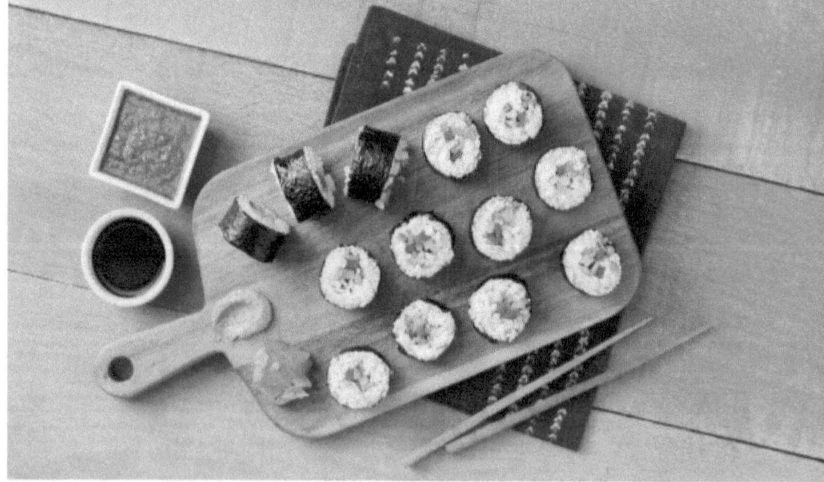

Instructions:

For the sushi rice:

1. Rinse the sushi rice in a fine-mesh strainer under cold water until the water runs clear. Then, drain and let it sit for about 30 minutes.

2. Cook the rice according to the package instructions. While it's cooking, in a small bowl, combine the rice vinegar, sugar, and salt. Gently warm it to dissolve the sugar and salt.

3. Once the rice is cooked and still warm, pour the vinegar mixture over it and gently fold it in, ensuring the rice is well coated with the dressing.

To assemble the rolls:

1. Place a bamboo rolling mat on a flat surface and cover it with a sheet of plastic wrap. Lay a sheet of nori seaweed on the mat with the rough side facing up.

2. Wet your hands to prevent the rice from sticking. Spread a thin layer of sushi rice over the nori, leaving about a 1 cm border at the top.

3. Place strips of avocado, cucumber, and carrot in the center of the rice.

4. Using the bamboo mat, start rolling the nori with the ingredients. Apply gentle pressure as you roll to ensure the sushi is compact.

5. With a slightly wet, sharp knife, cut the sushi roll into slices.

6. Serve the vegan sushi rolls with soy sauce, wasabi, and pickled ginger.

Cooking Tips:

- You can customize the ingredients of your sushi rolls with avocado, cucumber, carrot, or any other vegetable you like.

Nutritional Information (per serving, approximate):

- Calories: Approximately 150-200 kcal

- Protein: Approximately 3-4 g

- Fiber: Approximately 2-3 g

- Fat: Approximately 5-7 g

- Carbohydrates: Approximately 30-35 g

These Vegan Sushi Rolls are a delicious option for a light and healthy meal. We hope you enjoy making and eating your own sushi rolls!

Gluten-Free Oatmeal and Raisin Cookies

Ingredients:
- 1 cup of gluten-free oats
- 1/2 cup of almond flour (or almond meal)
- 1/4 cup of coconut flour
- 1/4 cup of coconut sugar (or your preferred sweetener)
- 1/2 teaspoon of cinnamon
- 1/4 teaspoon of salt
- 1/2 cup of raisins (or dried fruits of your choice)
- 1/4 cup of melted coconut oil
- 1 egg (or vegan egg substitute)
- 1 teaspoon of vanilla extract

Instructions:

1. Preheat your oven to 350°F (180°C) and line a baking sheet with parchment paper.

2. In a large bowl, combine the gluten-free oats, almond flour, coconut flour, coconut sugar, cinnamon, and salt.

3. Add the raisins (or dried fruits) to the dry ingredients and stir to distribute them evenly.

4. In a separate bowl, mix the melted coconut oil, egg (or vegan egg substitute), and vanilla extract.

5. Pour the wet mixture into the dry ingredients and mix until all the ingredients are well combined.

6. Using a cookie scoop or your hands, shape small dough balls and place them on the prepared baking sheet. Then, gently flatten each cookie with the back of a spoon.

7. Bake in the preheated oven for about 12-15 minutes, or until the cookies are golden around the edges.

8. Allow the cookies to cool on the baking sheet for a few minutes before transferring them to a wire rack to cool completely.

Cooking Tips:

- You can customize these cookies by adding chopped nuts, chocolate chips, or any other additional ingredient you like.

Nutritional Information (per cookie, approximate):

- Calories: Approximately 80-100 kcal

- Protein: Approximately 2-3 g

- Fiber: Approximately 1-2 g

- Fat: Approximately 6-8 g

- Carbohydrates: Approximately 6-8 g

These Gluten-Free Oatmeal and Raisin Cookies are a delightful option for a healthy snack. We hope you enjoy this recipe!

Baked Cauliflower Nuggets

Ingredients:
- 1 large cauliflower head, cut into florets
- 1 cup almond flour (or all-purpose flour if not gluten-free)
- 1 teaspoon garlic powder
- 1 teaspoon onion powder
- 1/2 teaspoon paprika
- 1/2 teaspoon cumin
- 1/2 teaspoon salt
- 1/4 teaspoon black pepper
- 1 cup plant-based milk (such as almond or soy milk)
- 1 cup breadcrumbs (ensure it's gluten-free if needed)
- Cooking spray

Instructions:

1. Preheat your oven to 425°F (220°C) and line a baking sheet with parchment paper.

2. In a large bowl, mix almond flour, garlic powder, onion powder, paprika, cumin, salt, and black pepper.

3. Dip each cauliflower floret into the plant-based milk and then coat it with the almond flour mixture.

4. Dip the cauliflower floret into the plant-based milk once more and then roll it in breadcrumbs.

5. Place the breaded cauliflower florets on the prepared baking sheet.

6. Spray the florets lightly with cooking spray to help them brown.

7. Bake in the preheated oven for about 25-30 minutes or until the cauliflower nuggets are golden and crispy.

8. Serve with your favorite dipping sauce, like vegan barbecue sauce, ketchup, or mustard.

Cooking Tips:

- You can adjust the seasonings and spices to your taste, add a little heat if you like bold flavors!

Nutritional Information (per serving, approximate):

- Calories: Approximately 150-200 kcal

- Protein: Approximately 5-6 g

- Fiber: Approximately 4-5 g

- Fat: Approximately 8-10 g

- Carbohydrates: Approximately 15-20 g

These Baked Cauliflower Nuggets are a delicious and healthy alternative to traditional chicken nuggets. We hope you enjoy this recipe!

Fruit and Spinach Smoothies

Ingredients:

   - 1 cup of fresh spinach

   - 1 cup of frozen fruits (such as strawberries, mango, pineapple, or your choice)

   - 1 ripe banana

   - 1 cup of plant-based milk (such as almond or soy milk)

   - 1 tablespoon of honey or maple syrup (optional)

   - Ice (optional)

   - Chia seeds or flax seeds (optional, for added nutrients)

Instructions:

1. Wash the spinach thoroughly and place it in the blender.

2. Add the frozen fruits to the blender. If you don't have frozen fruits, you can use fresh fruits and add ice to chill the smoothie.

3. Peel the banana and add it to the blender.

4. Pour the plant-based milk into the blender.

5. If you prefer extra sweetness, add a tablespoon of honey or maple syrup.

6. If you want to increase the fiber and nutrients, add a few teaspoons of chia seeds or flax seeds.

7. Blend all the ingredients until you have a smooth and consistent mixture. Add more milk for a thinner consistency or more ice for a colder smoothie.

Cooking Tips:

- You can customize your fruit and spinach smoothie with different fruits to suit your preferences.

Nutritional Information (per serving, approximate):

- Calories: Approximately 150-200 kcal
- Protein: Approximately 3-5 g
- Fiber: Approximately 4-6 g
- Fat: Approximately 2-4 g
- Carbohydrates: Approximately 30-35 g

These fruit and spinach smoothies are a delicious way to get a healthy dose of vegetables and fruits in your diet. We hope you enjoy this recipe!

Gluten-Free Oat Pancakes with Maple Syrup

Ingredients:
- 1 cup gluten-free oat flour
- 1 tablespoon sugar (or sweetener of your choice)
- 1 teaspoon gluten-free baking powder
- 1/2 teaspoon baking soda
- A pinch of salt
- 1 cup plant-based milk (such as almond or soy milk)
- 1 egg (or vegan egg substitute)
- 1 teaspoon vanilla extract
- Oil or vegan butter for greasing the pan

Instructions:

1. In a large bowl, combine gluten-free oat flour, sugar, gluten-free baking powder, baking soda, and salt.

2. In another bowl, mix plant-based milk, the egg (or vegan egg substitute), and vanilla extract.

3. Pour the liquid mixture into the dry ingredients and stir until you have a smooth batter.

4. Heat a non-stick skillet over medium heat and lightly grease it with oil or vegan butter.

5. Pour a small amount of batter into the hot skillet to form the pancakes. Cook until bubbles appear on the surface, then flip the pancake and cook the other side until golden brown.

6. Repeat this process with the remaining batter.

7. Serve the oat pancakes with maple syrup and your favorite fruits.

Cooking Tips:

- If you prefer thinner pancakes, you can add a bit more plant-based milk to the batter.

- Adding blueberries, sliced banana, or chopped nuts to the batter is a delicious way to customize your pancakes.

Nutritional Information (per serving, approximate, excluding maple syrup):

- Calories: Approximately 100-150 kcal

- Protein: Approximately 4-6 g

- Fiber: Approximately 2-3 g

- Fat: Approximately 2-4 g

- Carbohydrates: Approximately 15-20 g

These Gluten-Free Oat Pancakes are a delicious and gluten-free option for a healthy breakfast. We hope you enjoy this recipe!

Chocolate and Almond Energy Balls

Ingredients:
- 1 cup raw almonds
- 1 cup pitted dates
- 3 tablespoons unsweetened cocoa powder
- 1 teaspoon vanilla extract
- A pinch of salt
- 1/4 cup dark chocolate chips (make sure they're vegan if following a vegan diet)
- 1/4 cup rolled oats
- 2 tablespoons water (if needed)

Instructions:

1. Place the almonds in a food processor and pulse until they are crushed into small pieces.

2. Add the dates, cocoa powder, vanilla extract, and salt to the food processor. Process until the ingredients are well combined, and the mixture has a sticky texture.

3. If the mixture seems too dry, add water, one tablespoon at a time, until you achieve the right consistency.

4. Transfer the mixture to a bowl and add the dark chocolate chips and rolled oats. Mix well.

5. With slightly damp hands, form small balls from the mixture and place them on a tray or plate. Let the energy balls cool in the refrigerator for at least 30 minutes to firm up.

6. Once they're ready, you can store the energy balls in an airtight container in the refrigerator. They make for a healthy and energizing snack!

Cooking Tips:

- You can customize these energy balls by adding ingredients like shredded coconut, chia seeds, or chopped nuts.

Nutritional Information (per serving, approximate):

- Calories: Approximately 80-100 kcal per ball

- Protein: Approximately 2-3 g per ball

- Fiber: Approximately 2-3 g per ball

- Fat: Approximately 5-7 g per ball

- Carbohydrates: Approximately 6-8 g per ball

These Chocolate and Almond Energy Balls are a delicious and healthy snack, loaded with protein, fiber, and nutrients. We hope you enjoy them!

Mini Vegan Vegetable Quesadillas

Ingredients:
- 4 corn or wheat tortillas (ensure they are vegan)
- 1 cup red, green, and yellow bell peppers, sliced
- 1 cup red onion, sliced
- 1 cup mushrooms, sliced
- 1 cup fresh spinach
- 1 cup vegan shredded cheese (choose your favorite)
- Olive oil for cooking
- Salt and pepper to taste
- Guacamole and tomato sauce for serving (optional)

Instructions:

1. Heat a large skillet over medium-high heat and add a little olive oil.

2. Add the strips of bell peppers, onion, and mushrooms to the skillet. Sauté the vegetables until they are tender and slightly golden, seasoning with salt and pepper to taste.

3. While the vegetables are cooking, warm the tortillas in a separate skillet or in the oven so they are ready to fill.

4. On each tortilla, place a portion of fresh spinach, followed by a portion of the sautéed vegetables and a generous amount of vegan shredded cheese.

5. Fold the tortillas in half to create mini quesadillas and press gently.

6. Return the quesadillas to the hot skillet for a few minutes on each side until the cheese melts and the tortillas are golden and crispy.

7. Serve your mini vegan vegetable quesadillas with guacamole and tomato sauce if desired.

Cooking Tips:

- You can customize your quesadillas by adding ingredients like avocado, cilantro, or jalapeños.

Nutritional Information (per serving, approximate):

- Calories: Approximately 150-200 kcal per mini quesadilla

- Protein: Approximately 5-7 g per mini quesadilla

- Fiber: Approximately 3-4 g per mini quesadilla

- Fat: Approximately 5-7 g per mini quesadilla

- Carbohydrates: Approximately 20-25 g per mini quesadilla

These Mini Vegan Vegetable Quesadillas are a delicious and nutritious option for lunch or dinner. We hope you enjoy them!

Mini Broccoli and Carrot Patties
Ingredients:
- 2 cups broccoli, cut into small florets
- 1 cup grated carrots
- 1/2 cup red onion, finely chopped
- 1/4 cup chickpea flour (you can substitute with all-purpose flour if you don't need a gluten-free option)
- 1/4 cup breadcrumbs (ensure they are gluten-free if following a gluten-free diet)
- 2 cloves garlic, minced
- 1 teaspoon ground cumin
- 1/2 teaspoon paprika
- 2 tablespoons olive oil
- Salt and pepper to taste
- Oil for frying (you can use coconut oil or vegetable oil)
- Vegan yogurt sauce or hummus for serving (optional)

Instructions:
1. Steam the broccoli for a few minutes until it's tender but still crisp. Then, chop the broccoli florets into small pieces.

2. In a large bowl, combine the chopped broccoli, grated carrots, red onion, chickpea flour, breadcrumbs, minced garlic, ground cumin, paprika, olive oil, salt, and pepper. Mix all the ingredients until a uniform dough forms.

3. Heat enough oil in a large skillet over medium-high heat for frying the mini patties.

4. Take portions of the mixture and form small patties. Carefully place them in the hot skillet and fry until they are golden and crispy on both sides.

5. As the patties cook, place them on paper towels to remove excess oil.

6. Serve the Mini Broccoli and Carrot Patties with vegan yogurt sauce or hummus, if desired.

Cooking Tips:

- You can adjust the spices and seasonings to your taste. You can also add fresh herbs like cilantro or parsley for extra flavor.

Nutritional Information (per serving, approximate):

- Calories: Approximately 80-100 kcal per serving (varies depending on patty size)

- Protein: Approximately 3-4 g per serving

- Fiber: Approximately 2-3 g per serving

- Fat: Approximately 4-6 g per serving

- Carbohydrates: Approximately 10-12 g per serving

These Mini Broccoli and Carrot Patties are a delicious and healthy option for a snack or appetizer. We hope you enjoy them!

Gluten-Free Vegan Cereal Bars

Ingredients:
    - 2 cups gluten-free oats
    - 1 cup chopped walnuts or almonds
    - 1 cup dried fruits (such as raisins, blueberries, or dates), chopped
    - 1/2 cup maple syrup or agave syrup (for a completely vegan option)
    - 1/4 cup nut butter (such as almond or peanut butter)
    - 1 teaspoon vanilla extract
    - 1/2 teaspoon ground cinnamon
    - A pinch of salt

Instructions:

1. In a large skillet, toast the gluten-free oats over medium heat until they are lightly golden and fragrant. Stir constantly to prevent burning. Then, remove them from the heat and let them cool.

2. In a large bowl, combine the toasted oats, chopped walnuts or almonds, and dried fruits.

3. In a small saucepan over medium heat, warm the maple syrup (or agave syrup), nut butter, vanilla extract, ground cinnamon, and a pinch of salt. Stir until the mixture is smooth and well combined.

4. Pour the liquid mixture over the dry ingredients in the bowl and mix everything until well incorporated.

5. Transfer the mixture to a square or rectangular pan lined with parchment paper. Press the mixture firmly into the pan to compact it.

6. Let it cool in the refrigerator for at least 2 hours to allow the bars to firm up.

7. Once the bars are firm, remove them from the pan and cut them into bars of your desired size.

8. Store the Gluten-Free Vegan Cereal Bars in an airtight container in the refrigerator to maintain freshness.

Cooking Tips:

- You can customize these bars by adding ingredients like vegan chocolate chips, chia seeds, or shredded coconut.

Nutritional Information (per serving, approximate):

- Calories: Approximately 150-200 kcal per bar
- Protein: Approximately 4-5 g per bar
- Fiber: Approximately 3-4 g per bar
- Fat: Approximately 8-10 g per bar
- Carbohydrates: Approximately 15-20 g per bar

These Gluten-Free Vegan Cereal Bars are a healthy and delicious snack you can enjoy at any time. We hope you find them delightful!

Vegan Mini Potato Samosas

Ingredients:
For the filling:
- 2 medium potatoes, peeled and cubed
- 1/2 cup green peas (frozen peas are fine)
- 1 tablespoon cooking oil
- 1 teaspoon cumin seeds
- 1 teaspoon mustard seeds
- 1 teaspoon turmeric powder
- 1 teaspoon garam masala
- 1/2 teaspoon red chili powder (adjust to your preferred level of spiciness)
- Salt to taste
- 1 tablespoon fresh chopped cilantro
For the samosa dough:
- 1 cup wheat flour
- 2 tablespoons cooking oil
- Warm water, as needed to make the dough
- A pinch of salt

Instructions:

Preparing the filling:

1. Boil the potatoes in boiling water until they are tender. Drain and lightly mash them with a fork.

2. In a large skillet, heat the oil over medium heat. Add the mustard seeds and cumin seeds. When they begin to crackle, add the green peas and sauté for a few minutes.

3. Add the turmeric, garam masala, red chili powder, and salt. Stir well.

4. Incorporate the mashed potatoes and chopped cilantro. Cook for a few more minutes until all the ingredients are well combined. Remove from heat and let it cool.

Preparing the samosa dough:

1. In a large bowl, mix the wheat flour, oil, and a pinch of salt. Gradually add warm water and knead until you have a smooth and pliable dough. Cover the dough with a damp cloth and let it rest for 30 minutes.

Assembling the samosas:

1. Divide the dough into small walnut-sized balls. Roll each ball into a thin circle using a rolling pin.

2. Cut each circle in half to form two semicircles.

3. Take one semicircle of dough and shape it into a cone, sealing the edge with a little water.

4. Fill the cone with the potato and pea mixture.

5. Fold the cone upwards to seal the samosa into a triangular shape. Press the edges to ensure they are well sealed.

Frying the samosas:

1. Heat oil in a pan over medium heat. Once hot, fry the samosas until they are golden and crispy.

2. Remove the samosas with a slotted spoon and place them on a paper towel to remove excess oil.

Cooking Tips:

- You can adjust the level of spiciness by adding more or less red chili powder.

Nutritional Information (per serving, approximate):

- Calories: Approximately 100-120 kcal per samosa

- Protein: Approximately 2-3 g per samosa

- Fiber: Approximately 3-4 g per samosa

- Fat: Approximately 4-5 g per samosa

- Carbohydrates: Approximately 15-18 g per samosa

These Vegan Mini Potato Samosas are a delicious snack that you can enjoy on any occasion. We hope you enjoy them!

Dairy-Free Banana and Strawberry Ice Cream

Ingredients:

- 3 ripe bananas, frozen and sliced
- 1 cup fresh strawberries, washed and chopped
- 1/4 cup almond milk (or your choice of plant-based milk)
- 1 teaspoon vanilla extract
- 2 tablespoons maple syrup or agave syrup (optional, adjust to taste)

Instructions:

1. Freeze the banana slices for at least 2 hours or until completely frozen.

2. In a blender or food processor, place the frozen banana slices and the strawberries.

3. Add the almond milk, vanilla extract, and maple syrup (if desired).

4. Blend everything on high speed until the mixture is smooth and creamy. You may need to stop the blender or processor several times to scrape down the sides and ensure everything is well mixed.

5. Taste the ice cream and adjust the sweetness to your liking by adding more maple syrup if needed.

6. Transfer the ice cream to an airtight container and place it in the freezer for at least 1 hour to achieve a firmer texture.

7. Serve the Dairy-Free Banana and Strawberry Ice Cream in cones or cups, and garnish it with fresh strawberries if desired.

Cooking Tips:

- You can experiment with other fruits instead of strawberries, such as blueberries, mango, or raspberries, to create different ice cream flavors.

- Ensure that the fruits are frozen before making the ice cream to achieve the desired texture.

Nutritional Information (per serving, approximate):

- Calories: Approximately 100-120 kcal per serving

- Protein: Approximately 1-2 g per serving

- Fiber: Approximately 3-4 g per serving

- Fat: Approximately 0.5-1 g per serving

- Carbohydrates: Approximately 25-30 g per serving

This Dairy-Free Banana and Strawberry Ice Cream is a refreshing and healthy option to satisfy your dessert cravings. We hope you enjoy it!

Vegan Chocolate Cookies with Chocolate Chips

Ingredients:
- 1 cup all-purpose flour (or almond flour for a gluten-free version)
- 1/3 cup unsweetened cocoa powder
- 1/2 teaspoon baking soda
- 1/4 teaspoon salt
- 1/2 cup brown sugar
- 1/4 cup melted coconut oil (or vegetable oil)
- 1/4 cup almond milk (or another plant-based milk)
- 1 teaspoon vanilla extract
- 1/2 cup vegan chocolate chips (ensure they are dairy-free)

Instructions:

1. Preheat your oven to 180°C (350°F) and line a baking sheet with parchment paper.

2. In a large bowl, mix the flour, cocoa powder, baking soda, and salt.

3. In another bowl, combine the brown sugar, melted coconut oil, almond milk, and vanilla extract.

4. Pour the wet mixture into the dry mixture and stir until a dough forms.

5. Add the vegan chocolate chips and mix until they are evenly distributed in the dough.

6. Using an ice cream scoop or your hands, form small dough balls and place them on the prepared baking sheet. Slightly flatten each ball with the back of a fork to shape them into cookies.

7. Bake the cookies in the preheated oven for 10-12 minutes or until the edges are firm.

8. Remove the cookies from the oven and let them cool on the baking sheet for a few minutes before transferring them to a cooling rack to cool completely.

Cooking Tips:

- You can adjust the amount of chocolate chips to your preference. Add more if you love chocolate.

- If the dough seems too sticky, you can refrigerate it for a few minutes before forming the cookie balls.

Nutritional Information (per cookie, approximate):

- Calories: Approximately 80-100 kcal per cookie

- Protein: Approximately 1-2 g per cookie

- Fiber: Approximately 1-2 g per cookie

- Fat: Approximately 4-6 g per cookie

- Carbohydrates: Approximately 9-12 g per cookie

These Vegan Chocolate Cookies with Chocolate Chips are a treat for chocolate lovers and are perfect for any occasion. We hope you enjoy them!

Throughout this book, we've guided you on a culinary journey filled with delightful flavors and creativity in the kitchen. We've explored recipes that are healthy, delicious, and, most importantly, suitable for children with gluten-free and vegan diets.

Each recipe has been crafted with love and care, using ingredients that are eco-friendly and beneficial for health. We've taken the youngest palates into consideration while keeping simplicity in mind to make the recipes easy to prepare at home.

Let's remember that cooking is a way to nourish the body and soul, and these recipes demonstrate that healthy and delicious can go hand in hand. Feed your little gourmets with love, nutrition, and the wonder of exploring new flavors.

Thank you for joining us on this culinary journey. Here's a recipe book filled with love, flavor, and fun. We hope you enjoy preparing and sharing these delicious recipes with your little gourmets!

Bon appétit, and may the culinary adventure continue!

Don't miss out!

Visit the website below and you can sign up to receive emails whenever BDM publishes a new book. There's no charge and no obligation.

https://books2read.com/r/B-A-UZKJ-YQLPC

BOOKS 2 READ

Connecting independent readers to independent writers.

Did you love *30 Vegan Recipes for Kids Gluten Free*? Then you should read *Vegan Recipes Cookbook - 30 Vegan Desserts*[1] by BDM!

Are you ready to embark on a delightful journey into the world of plant-based sweetness? Look no further than "Vegan Recipes Cookbook - 30 Vegan Desserts," where we invite you to savor a collection of delectable and guilt-free dessert creations that will revolutionize the way you think about vegan baking.

In this cookbook, we've curated a selection of 30 irresistible dessert recipes that showcase the boundless possibilities of vegan cooking. From luscious chocolate brownies to refreshing fruit-infused tarts, each recipe has been meticulously crafted to bring you the perfect balance of flavor and health.

---

1. https://books2read.com/u/3LxvgX

2. https://books2read.com/u/3LxvgX

What Awaits You in "Vegan Recipes Cookbook - 30 Vegan Desserts"?

- **Healthy Indulgence:** Dive into a world where dessert indulgence meets nutritional goodness. Our recipes are crafted with natural, whole ingredients, free from refined sugars and dairy, offering you a guilt-free experience.

- **Ease of Cooking:** Whether you're a seasoned chef or a newbie in the kitchen, our recipes are designed to be user-friendly and accessible to all skill levels. Follow along with clear, step-by-step instructions and discover the joy of hassle-free baking.

- **A Symphony of Flavors:** From timeless classics that evoke comfort to innovative creations that ignite your taste buds, you'll find a diverse array of sweet options to cater to every craving and occasion.

- **Culinary and Nutritional Insights:** Throughout the cookbook, you'll find valuable cooking tips and insights, as well as nutritional information for each dessert. Learn the art of plant-based baking and make informed choices about your food.

With "Vegan Recipes Cookbook - 30 Vegan Desserts," you're not just embarking on a culinary adventure; you're also contributing to a more sustainable and compassionate world. Each recipe represents a step towards a healthier and ethically-driven lifestyle.

Are you ready to satisfy your sweet cravings while aligning with your values? Dive into the world of cruelty-free baking and discover that vegan desserts can be equally, if not more, delicious than their traditional counterparts.

Embrace the joy of plant-based desserts today. Grab your copy and start baking your vegan dreams into reality!